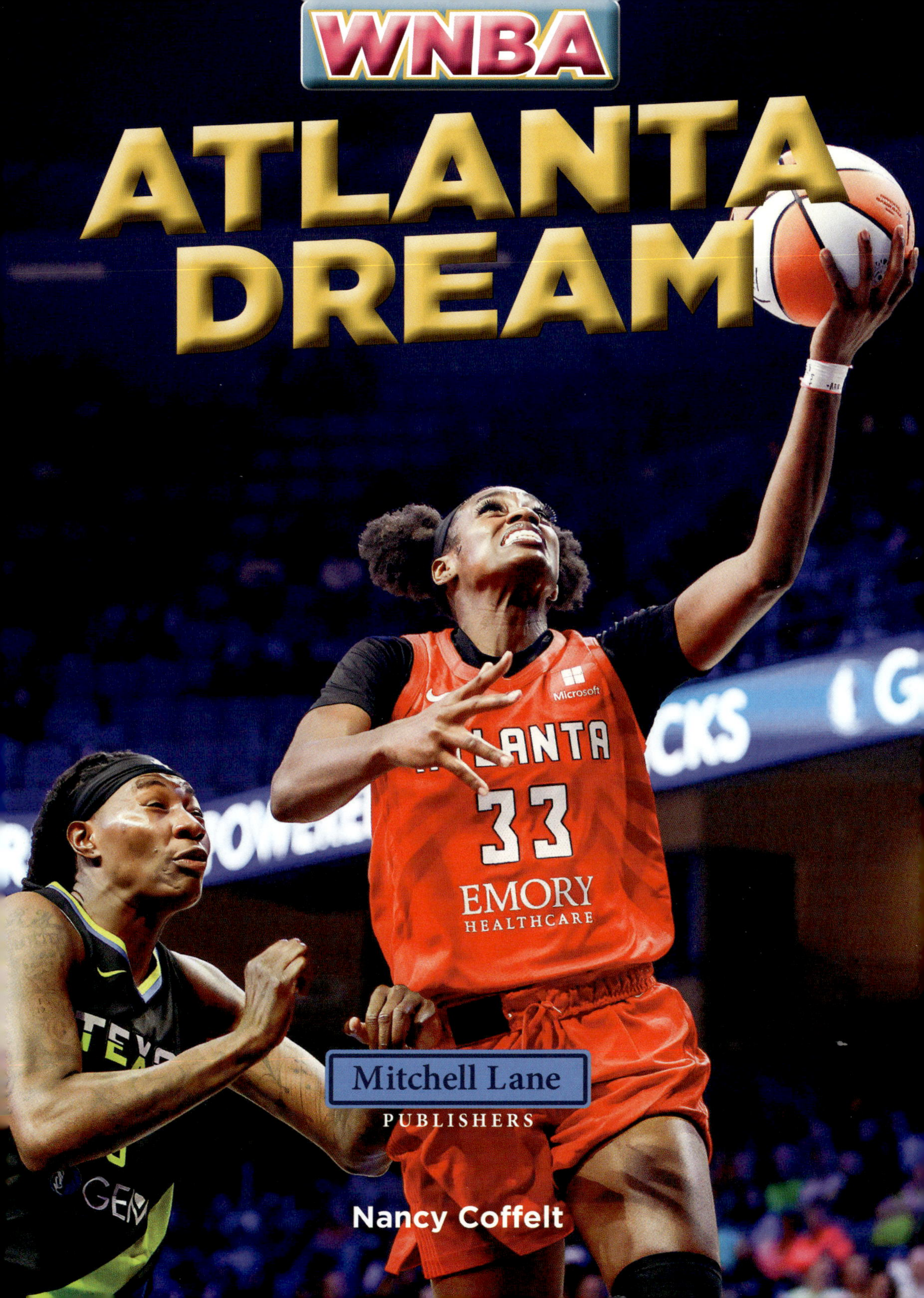
WNBA
ATLANTA DREAM
Microsoft
33
EMORY
HEALTHCARE
Mitchell Lane
PUBLISHERS
Nancy Coffelt

Mitchell Lane
PUBLISHERS

mitchelllanepub.com

2001 SW 31st Avenue
Hallandale, FL 33009

First Edition, 2026.
Author: Nancy Coffelt
Designer: Ed Morgan
Editor: Tammy Gagne

Series: WNBA
Title: Atlanta Dream

Library bound ISBN: 979-8-89260-474-1
eBook ISBN: 979-8-89260-497-0

Photo credits: p. 9, 11, 13, 17, 19 newscom.com;
balance Alamy

CONTENTS

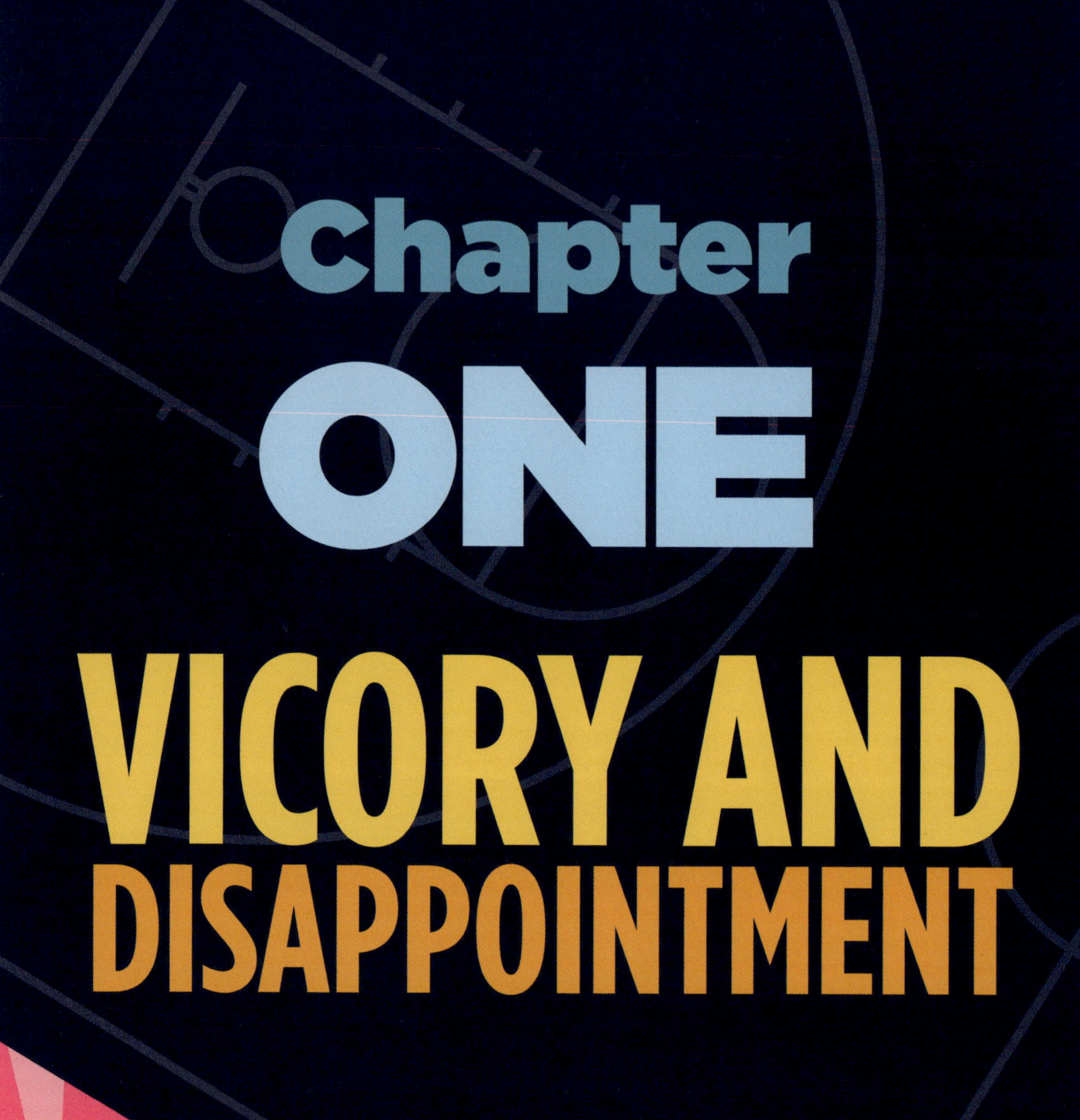
Chapter
ONE
VICORY AND
DISAPPOINTMENT

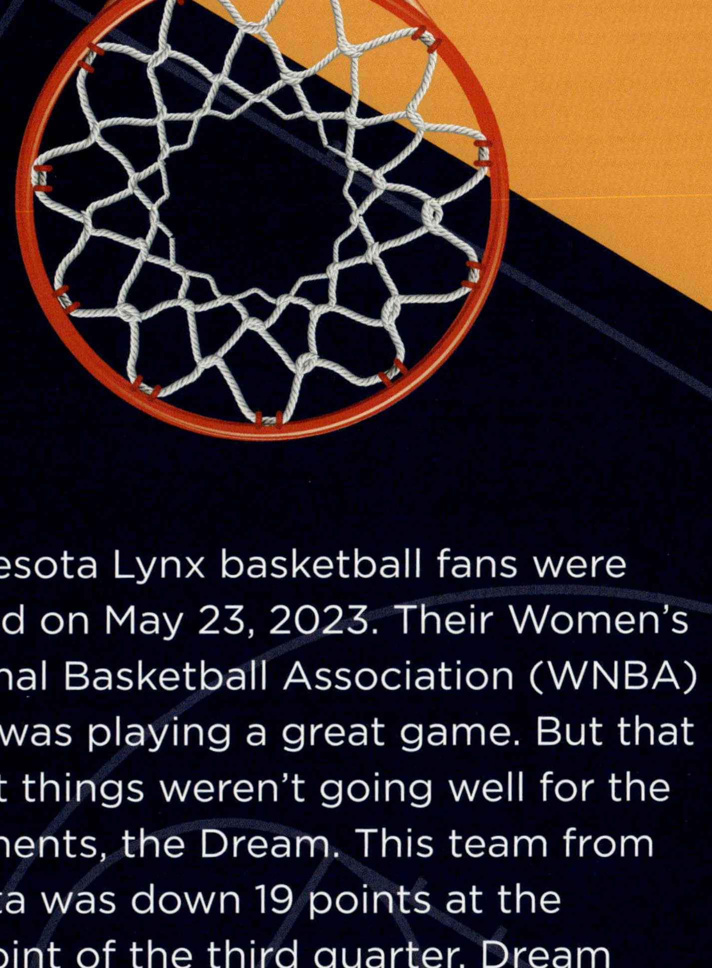

Minnesota Lynx basketball fans were excited on May 23, 2023. Their Women's National Basketball Association (WNBA) team was playing a great game. But that meant things weren't going well for the opponents, the Dream. This team from Atlanta was down 19 points at the midpoint of the third quarter. Dream forward Naz Hillmon caught her breath and quickly surveyed Target Arena. The Dream appeared to be facing a huge loss. Something had to change. "We pride ourselves on defense, and we knew it wasn't up to our standards in the first half," Hillmon told reporters.

CHAPTER ONE

Change was about to come. Hillmon and her teammates stepped up their game. The Dream players started communicating better. That stopped the Lynx's **advancement**. Hillmon scored 13 points in the second half. Dream guard Allisha Gray racked up 26 points for the game. It looked like Dream guard Aari McDonald would score just 6 points. But that was about to change, too. McDonald sunk a three-pointer in the last minute. The Dream pulled ahead to win the game with a final score of 83–77. At one time, the Atlanta team had been behind a whopping 19 points. It was the largest comeback in the history of the **franchise**.

Victory and Disappointment

FAST FACT

Dream player Rhyne Howard was named to the 2023 WNBA All-Star Game. Her team won the game with a final score of 143–127.

CHAPTER ONE

The Dream began the next season with a 92–81 win against the Los Angeles Sparks. Strong defense helped the Dream keep control. "I'm really happy that we were able to come in and get a win," head coach Tanisha Wright told the *Peachtree Hoops* website. "LA is always a team that plays us super tough and **aggressive**." But by July 2024, the Dream was struggling. A loss to the Lynx added to the team's losing streak of eight straight games. It put the Dream in ninth place in the league and out of the 2024 playoffs.

Victory and Disappointment

Former Atlanta Dream head coach, Tanisha Wright started her WNBA career playing for the Seattle Storm.

Chapter TWO

A NAME TO INSPIRE

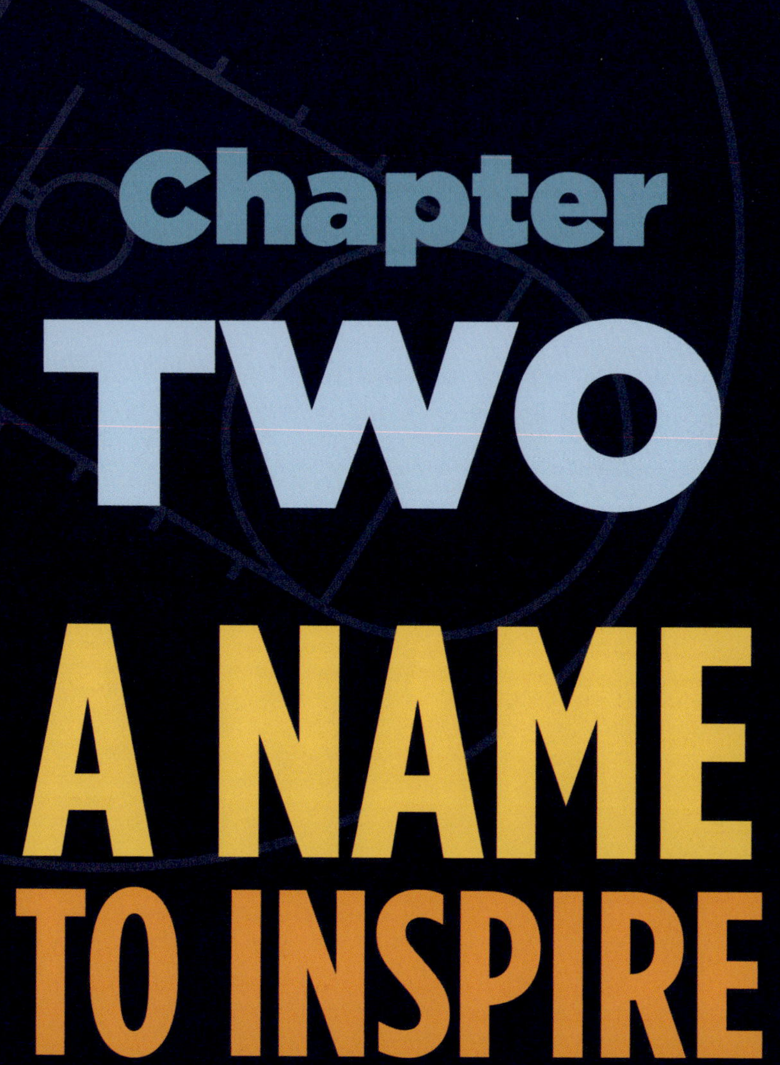

WNBA President Donna Orender (left), Atlanta owner Kathy Betty (middle), and former Dream owner J. Ron Terwilliger

The WNBA was founded in 1996. At that time, there were just eight teams in the league. By 2007, there were thirteen. Ron Terwilliger made Atlanta the home of the fourteenth team in 2008.

CHAPTER TWO

With seating for about 18,000 women's basketball fans, Philips Arena became the **venue** for the team's home games. The team also needed a name. Terwilliger considered the name Stars. But it didn't convey the message he wanted.

The late Reverend Martin Luther King Jr. provided inspiration. On August 28, 1963, the civil rights leader gave a speech that included the phrase *I have a dream*. The address stressed that dreams could be achieved through **solidarity**. It was the perfect message for the new team.

"Atlanta is a city of dreamers and this week we have had time to reflect on what it means to dream and what can happen when you do," Terwilliger told the WNBA's *LiveJournal* website. "We believe Dream best captures Atlanta's spirit and the core values of the WNBA. We look forward to the Atlanta Dream continuing to make history as we work toward our goal of **transcending** sports."

A Name to Inspire

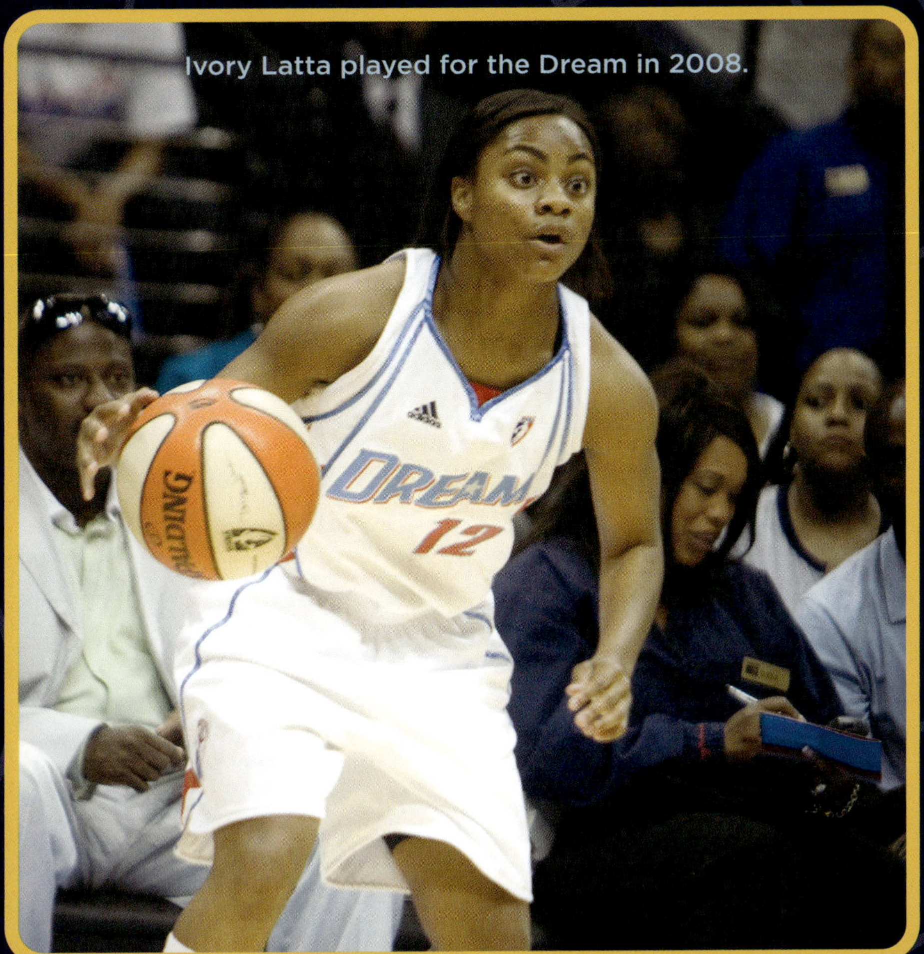

Ivory Latta played for the Dream in 2008.

FAST FACT

The Dream won its first game on July 5, 2008. The team beat the Chicago Sky in overtime, 91–84.

CHAPTER TWO

In 2017, Philips Arena received a $200 million makeover. The venue was renamed State Farm Arena at this time. Three years later, there was another change for the Dream when the team moved to Gateway Center Arena in College Park. The Dream wanted to stay in downtown Atlanta. But the team was drawing fewer than 4,500 attendees at each game.

Though popular, the Dream just couldn't fill State Farm Arena's seats. But the team *could* fill Gateway's 3,500 seats. Ticket sales for the 2024 season confirmed that the move was a smart one for the team. Season tickets sold out. By the end of April, five games had sold out as well. The fans were still behind their Dream team.

A Name to Inspire

Guard Allisha Gray was named an All-Star for the first time on July 2, 2024.

Chapter THREE

COACHING MOVES

Marynell Meadors (left) with player Angel McCoughtry

Even before he founded the Dream, owner Ron Terwilliger was committed to hiring a female coach. He told ESPN, "We'd prefer to have a women's coach since it's a women's league." He hired Marynell Meadors for the position. Meadors coached the Dream for four years.

CHAPTER THREE

Three more head coaches served in the role before Tanisha Wright, joined the Dream. A former WNBA player, Wright led the team from 2021 to 2024. When she took the job, she became the fifth Black coach in the WNBA.

Wright grew up playing basketball whenever she got the chance. In middle school she and her friends would sneak games in before school. After school, they headed back to the neighborhood court to play some more.

"We didn't waste a second. We played in every element: rain, snow, and thick summer heat. It didn't matter. Basketball is what kept us out of trouble," Wright wrote on *The Player's Tribune* website. She went on to play college ball at Penn State. In 2005, she was drafted by the WNBA's Seattle Storm.

FAST FACT

Atlanta Dream Coach Nicki Collen was named WNBA Coach of the Year in 2018. It was her first year serving as head coach of the team.

CHAPTER THREE

In 2023, Wright brought the Dream to the playoffs for the first time since 2018. She earned the Associated Press Coach of the Year award that year. Excitement about the playoffs kept growing. The Dream began the 2024 season with a sellout crowd at Gateway Center.

Wright was fiercely committed to the game and the team. "I tell them all the time . . . when you're the hardest working, toughest team, I don't care who we play, we'll always be in a position to win games," Wright told *The Next* website in 2022.

Karl Smesko took over as head coach ahead of the 2025 season. He came to Atlanta after spending twenty-three years coaching at Florida Gulf Coast University. He hopes to take the Dream all the way to the championships.

Coaching Moves

Tanisha Wright helped the Storm with a win over the Mystics on August 25, 2009.

Chapter FOUR

THE DREAM CONTINUES

Tina Charles

The Atlanta Dream is filled with talented players. On June 8, 2024, Dream center Tina Charles played her 400th career game. The thirty-five-year-old **dominated** the opposing team, the Chicago Sky. Following the Dream's win, Charles led all scorers with 22 points in the game. She also achieved her 1,050th career rebound.

CHAPTER FOUR

Charles played college ball for the University of Connecticut. After playing for several other WNBA teams, she joined the Dream in 2024. "Tina's ability to score and rebound the basketball at an **elite** level immediately helps this basketball team," general manager Dan Padover stated in a 2024 press release.

At 6 feet, 2 inches (1.9 m) tall, guard Rhyne Howard came to the Dream after playing for Kentucky University. She quickly made her mark by being named the 2022 Rookie of the Year. In July 2023, Howard made WNBA history. She became the youngest player to score more than 40 points in a single game with a total of 43. "It felt great," Howard told **sideline reporter** Autumn Johnson after the game. "And it just kept flowing."

The Dream Continues

FAST FACT

Five-time WNBA All-Star Angel McCoughtry played for the Atlanta Dream for 10 seasons, beginning in 2009 when she was the team's first overall draft pick.

CHAPTER FOUR

Cheyenne Parker-Tyus was drafted by the Chicago Sky from Middle Tennessee State in 2015. The 6-feet, 4-inch (1.9-m) forward signed with the Dream in 2021. In an interview on the Atlanta Dream's website, Parker-Tyus said, "The Dream has endless **potential** and I'm excited to be a part of that." In 2024, she was included in ESPN's Top 25 WNBA Players of the Year.

Members of the Atlanta team continue to make their dreams come true. They ended their 2024 season with sellout crowds. They ranked fifth in the 2024 conference standings.

Morgan Shaw Parker is the team's current president. She told Atlanta's WXIA, "What's happening this year is not just about one person, one team, or one season." Parker said she sees it as the **culmination** of everyone's hard work. "All the women that came before us who really put the sport on the map."

The Dream Continues

Forward Cheyenne Parker-Tyus had to sit out the last part of the 2024 season with an ankle injury.

GLOSSARY

advancement
The action of progressing toward a goal

aggressive
Playing in a way to dominate

culmination
The realization of a goal

dominated
Controlled by being more skilled or powerful

elite
Superior in skills and ability

franchise
A team in a professional sport league

potential
The ability to be successful in the future

solidarity
Unity created by a common goal

sideline reporter
A journalist who interviews players and coaches from a game's venue

transcending
Rising above or moving beyond

venue
A building or space where a game takes place

SLAM DUNK WNBA TRIVIA

- With its first-ever draft pick, the Atlanta Dream chose Tamera Young in the 2008 WNBA Draft. She was traded to the Chicago Sky the following year.
- The Dream made it into the playoffs for the first time in 2010. They lost all three games of the finals to the Seattle Storm.
- Drafted by the Atlanta Dream in 2012, Tiffany Hayes went on to play in 328 games, the most of any player in the franchise's history.
- In 2016, the Atlanta Dream had one of the biggest comebacks in basketball history. After trailing the Seattle Storm by 26 points, the Dream won the game with a final score of 77–64.
- In 2017, Dream point guard Layshia Clarendon became the first Dream player named MVP of the WNBA All-Star Game.
- Renee Montgomery became the first former WNBA player to own a team in 2021. Montgomery played for the Atlanta Dream from 2018 to 2020.

FIND OUT MORE

IN PRINT

Helt, Julianna. *Minnesota Lynx*. Mitchell Lane Publishers, 2026.

Howell, Izzi. *Martin Luther King Jr.* Crabtree Publishing Company, 2021.

Leed, Percy. *Basketball's NBA and WNBA Finals*. Lerner Publications, 2025.

ON THE INTERNET

Atlanta Dream.
https://dream.wnba.com.

"Atlanta Dream," ***ESPN*****, n.d.**
www.espn.com/wnba/team/_/name/atl/atlanta-dream.

"Atlanta Dream," ***FOX Sports*****, n.d.**
www.foxsports.com/wnba/atlanta-dream-team-roster.

INDEX

About the Author

Nancy Coffelt has never played professional basketball, but she did win a free-throw contest in junior high school. Nancy lives, writes, and paints in eastern Oregon. She appreciates athletes and anyone else who follow their dreams and work hard to achieve their goals.